MW01243631

# Bhagavad Gita
A distraught man's conversation with God.

\* \* \*

Translation by Richard Lawrence
RichardLawrenceWrites@gmail.com

\* \* \*

Second Edition -- ©2014

# Table of Contents

# Introduction

The Bhagavad Gita, the Song of God, composed over 2000 years ago, is the story of a man's dilemma during a family feud. In the middle of impending violence, he is desperately confused about whether he should participate in the bloodshed. God, in the form of his charioteer, explains the nature of life to this distraught archer, eventually extinguishing his fears. And as a witness to this conversation, we the audience receive insight into our own existence, and develop an understanding of the world and our place within it.

# Chapter 1

The old blind king asks of his servant: What is happening in the field of battle, where my sons and nephews gather to fight?

His servant, gifted with divine vision, replies: I see your eldest son approaching his teacher of warfare, remarking, "Although many great warriors fill the ranks of my cousins' army, our army is greater." Then, as to instill confidence, the eldest of the clan roars like a lion, followed by a blast of his horn, signaling a readiness for battle, setting off a clangor of horns and drums from the entire army.

Across the battlefield, upon hearing the clamor of the opposition, the Archer and his Charioteer blow their own horns, inspiring their army to make a sound so thunderous as to inject fear into the hearts of their adversaries.

Sensing the fight is soon to begin, the Archer instructs his Charioteer: Bring us between these two great armies so that I may observe all who are assembled for battle.

While surveying the scene, the Archer is struck with the awareness that his kinsmen, friends, and teachers are on both sides.

This realization fills the Archer with a great sorrow, causing him to say: Charioteer, I grow weak and unable to stand, how can I wish for my kindred to be destroyed? Victory would bring emptiness, how could I enjoy life after killing my kinsmen? It is a crime against our family and every generation that follows. At the very least, I would rather lay down my weapons and be slain by the other side, than participate in this wicked act.

Overwhelmed with grief, the Archer drops his bow and sinks down into his chariot, his eyes filled with tears.

# Chapter 2

His Charioteer responds: Why such weakness in a time of war? Stand and fight!

The Archer replies: How can I fight against my eldest family member that I dearly love, or my mentor that so faithfully trained me in warfare and receives my utmost respect, or any of my family and friends? Is it better to conquer or be defeated? Even receiving unrivaled wealth and power would fail to appease my sorrow if I should kill those I love. Please Charioteer, I am confused, advise me. I will not fight!

His Charioteer, smiling, says: Your grief is pointless. These men have always existed and will never cease to exist. Just as our essence travels through infancy, youth, and old age, it will travel through another body.

The senses provide a means to experience the temporary aspects of life, so have patience as these events come and go. But the unchanging underlying reality will always exist, it cannot be destroyed by any means, everything else is mere illusion. Although your body may appear to perish, your essence is eternal and cannot be harmed, therefore fight this battle!

As tattered garments are discarded and replaced with

new ones, so too does your essence exchange bodies. As death is certain for those that are born, so too is birth certain for those that die.

As a man of action, you are inclined to participate in this battle, it is what you've been trained for, it is your duty. Failing to perform your natural tendencies will ultimately result in deep dissatisfaction. Therefore, great Archer, arise and fight!

Furthermore, those who would claim that ultimate understanding and bliss only come from performing rituals described by tradition and sacred texts, are misled. The most ancient and sacred ritual, is life itself. What use is a collection of water when it flows from everywhere? So too is a collection of sacred rituals of little value when the world itself is sacred. But what is always useful and never a waste, is performing action that suits you.

Do not wish for a life of inaction, and do not be motivated by reward, simply perform your role. Do not be concerned with the results of action, your attitude should remain constant through success and failure. Seeing through delusion, realize that actions and outcomes are without value. Ultimate joy comes to those that stop chasing imaginary rewards. Wisdom comes to those utilizing discipline to maintain a steady attitude.

The Archer responds: Charioteer, please describe such

a one that achieves an unchanging attitude through discipline.

The Charioteer replies: Such a man is satisfied, requiring nothing. He does not seek pleasure, is undisturbed by suffering, and does not know fear or anger, realizing that all outcomes are the same. And though they may deluge his mind, he controls his thoughts with discipline, focusing on that which never changes.

Dwelling on objects perceived by the senses increases fondness and craving for them, eventually resulting in frustration and confusion. A disciplined man engages with the perceptible world without needing to grasp it tightly, realizing its illusionary nature and impermanence. He therefore engages calmly, confidently, and joyfully.

If left undisciplined, controlled by the perception of the senses, the mind is swept away like a ship subjected to a storm. And as the ocean's depths are undisturbed even as rivers rush in, so too is a disciplined man at peace when thoughts and emotions flood his mind. Free of delusion, his essence found, he experiences joy.

# Chapter 3

Overwhelmed, the confused Archer asks: If disciplining my mind to appreciate life's nature is a means to end my suffering, why must I participate in this dreadful act?

The Charioteer responds: One cannot refrain from action. To exist is to act, if only to sustain the body. Natural tendencies compel action -- but one can detach from the performance by utilizing reason to reinforce that the senses perceive only illusion.

Performing necessary action is better than inaction. Nor is it right to restrain the body while the mind is filled with want. Follow your nature, performing without concern for outcomes or rewards, this is freedom. Acting out your role, whatever it may be, is a celebration of life itself, it is the greatest good. Not performing your role, by chasing the seemingly pleasant, while avoiding the seemingly unpleasant, is an unfulfilled life.

Ambitions and goals being unnecessary, find delight and contentment internally while externally performing what must be done. Relentlessly, the universe churns without purpose or concern for reward, acting for the sake of action, a role-model for that which lives within. Failing to act, all would collapse. Performing your duty, without chasing reward or avoiding unpleasantness, preserves the world.

But below the surface, the forces of nature are the true source of action, not the individual. Realizing that one's essence is not the originator of action, but a witness to life, allows detachment from action, otherwise one is trapped by delusion, attached to one's actions. So do not attempt to gain or retain your hopes through action, maintain in your mind the realization of your essence and its nature, and then act. Fight this battle!

Following nature's path, trusting it without complaint, attain freedom. Every creature adheres to its nature, there is no value in restraint. Your role, performed imperfectly, is better than another's performed perfectly. Attraction and aversion are part of everything that engages the senses, overcome this obstacle and succumb to neither.

The Archer asks: Charioteer, what drives a person to perform vile acts against his own wishes?

The Charioteer responds: It is the desire for something specific to occur and the related frustration. Desire obscures truth and hinders reasoning, causing confusion. Fight and destroy this insatiable enemy, desire. Guided by your essence, discipline the mind so it cannot be fooled by what the senses perceive, which is only delusion.

# Chapter 4

The Charioteer proclaims: In the beginning, I taught this timeless discipline to the ancients. But as ages passed, the knowledge faded. What I have taught you this day, as my friend and disciple, is this ancient wisdom.

The confused Archer replies: By your appearance, you are not that old, how could you have taught this philosophy so long ago?

The Charioteer responds: We have many lives, I remember mine, you do not. Whenever disorder reigns in this world, I come into being, rebalancing life, protecting the best aspects while destroying the worst. I am the beacon for the fulfillment of one's duty. He who appreciates my divine nature, comes to me.

As men commit themselves to following the path towards me, I commit to them. No longer clinging to this world, lacking fear and frustration, focusing their thoughts on me, they reach me.

Appreciate activity, not outcomes, and be content. Subdue your hopes, refrain from expecting a particular result, and be pleased by whatever comes. When following your natural tendencies, performing your role, engaging in life without selfish motive, free from envy, unconcerned with how consequences will affect you, content with any outcome, you attain freedom. Unattached to your actions, you are no longer bound to this world, you come to me.

Performing action without attachment is how you display your devotion to me. Even those performing the worst of actions can be freed by this knowledge. Just as fire turns wood to ash, this knowledge turns all action to ash.

Devoted and focused, refining your thoughts, find peace. Conquer your obsession for earthly delights -- mere illusions which can never be grasped -- through the practice of discipline, severing all doubt by the knowledge of your essence. Implement this discipline and stand up!

# Chapter 5

The Archer asks: Should I solve my problem by physically engaging with the world or by finding a thought-based solution, reshaping how I think?

The Charioteer replies: Only the unwise separate the two, as one is necessary for the other. With discipline, a man reins in his thoughts -- weeding out the negativity, he unites his essence with the essence of all, and when he acts, he is blameless and unconcerned whether a particular outcome is attained.

Through practice, a man may repeatedly remind himself, until it becomes ingrained in his thinking, that he is not the originator of action. It is not he that makes the eyes see, the ears listen, the skin feel, the nose smell, the mouth taste, the body sleep, or the lungs breathe, these events occur automatically, without intervention.

While engaging with the world, he reminds himself: it is the senses alone that perceive external objects. Observing himself, he realizes he is not the driver, but the passenger, and abandons his misguided desire to manipulate the world. With faith in his nature, his motivations are pure, and he achieves peace.

The forces of nature alone are what instigate action and provide the resulting fruit. The power that brought this world into being does not instigate the actions of mankind nor cause mankind to act rightly or wrongly. Delusion comes from not knowing one's essence.

The knowledge of one's essence, like the sun, illuminates the truth of the world. With this vision, all creatures and classes of mankind are seen equally, united by a common core. An esteemed priest, a societal outcast, a cow, an elephant, and a dog, are all parts of the whole. And having overcome the delusion of separateness, realizing the flawless balance of life, only tranquility remains.

Do not look upon this world judgmentally, celebrating what you perceive as pleasant while protesting what you perceive as unpleasant. Know the underlying union of all.

Do not be attached to this world, seeking satisfaction from temporary illusions. Train your thoughts on the eternal and know joy.

He who dissolves every surge of desire and anger is disciplined, calm, and full of joy. Mastering his mind, he removes all doubts, and sees the positive aspects in all creatures. Dedicated to this path, focused on the breath, blocking out the external, bringing thoughts under control, melting away desire, fear, and anger -- he finds freedom.

Knowing me as the enjoyer of one's efforts, and friend to all, he attains peace.

# Chapter 6

The Charioteer continues: Do not devise intricate schemes for your life, simply perform what your role dictates, doing what must be done, while at the same time abandoning your selfish attitude, renouncing the idea that actions should be pursued or avoided based on personal gratification -- this is discipline.

Participation in life provides a means to practice this discipline. And upon maturation, this discipline leads to tranquility, a state attained when one's deliberate attempts to satisfy selfish wants have been abandoned, while at the same time engaged in the world lightheartedly, as if a fictional tale.

Utilize the reasoning mind to cultivate joy and tranquility, not as a means to indulge in negativity. Depending on its focus, the mind becomes the best friend or the worst enemy.

A disciplined mind remains the same in chill and warmth, distress and delight, rejection and praise. As the illusions of this world attempt to ensnare, the disciplined mind is beyond reach, confident and content. Worldly objects are of equal value, nothing is treasured. Well trained is the mind that views others without distinction, impartial to all.

With a mind separate from the external world, free of desire for worldly objects and outcomes, continually practice this mental discipline: remaining motionless, in a position free from strain but not easy for sleep, observe the mind, restrain from focusing on fleeting thoughts or the perceptions of the senses, continuously return focus to that which endures. From this practice, one's essence is freed of its fetters.

Calm and free of fear, watching and guiding the mind, focusing on the eternal, become one with the everlasting. A controlled mind finds tranquility.

Eating too much or too little, sleeping too much or too little, these represent a lack of discipline. Sorrow comes to an end through the practice of restraint. For this reason, regulate diet, sleep, activity, and recreation.

Untroubled by the external world, with an attitude of detachment, without wants, one is disciplined. Such a mind does not waver, like a flame shielded from the wind. With rampant thoughts diminished through practice, one's essence is revealed, and contentment thrives.

The realization that truth does not exist in the realm of the senses, brings supreme joy. When understood, one remains in this state, and never strays, knowing there is nothing greater, unshaken by any affliction.

Discipline is the method to cut one's connection to suffering, knowing this, practice with determination. Do not allow the mind to imagine frivolous wants -- abandon wants, use the reasoning mind to dismantle what the senses perceive. Over time, no longer focused on the external, this practice results in tranquility.

When the mind wanders down an unfavorable path, observe it, bring awareness back to the mind itself, ceasing to follow the volatile thoughts. A mind made tranquil through the practice of discipline, harmonizes with the eternal.

No longer swayed by the perceptions of the senses, and without wants, the untroubled mind fills with joy. Seeing all things equally, one experiences a fellowship with all, realizing the essence of life is within all. One who sees his essence everywhere is never lost.

Seeing one's self in all things, whether delightful or dreadful, is one who is well disciplined.

The troubled Archer, confused, says: You speak of stillness of mind, but I am struggling, my mind can not keep still, it is chaotic, fierce, and persistent. It seems impossible to rein in, as if trying to restrain the wind.

The Charioteer responds: Indeed, the mind is turbulent and difficult to control, but dedicated practice and a detached perspective can restrain it. One who strives to attain this discipline can achieve it.

Again troubled, the Archer asks: But what of the man that attempts, yet fails to attain a disciplined mind, is he not a double failure? Failing first in this life, and then in death -- where does he end up? Please answer, and end my confusion.

The Charioteer responds: One that pursues a disciplined approach to life cannot go wrong. In the next life, he is reborn at the level previously attained, his essence imprinted with past understanding. Birth after birth, striving towards perfection through discipline, he ultimately unites with the infinite. Therefore, devote yourself to governing the mind.

# Chapter 7

The Charioteer continues: Know me as your guide upon this path of discipline, keeping me in your thoughts. Now hear me, as I explain the way in which to know me -- once realized, there is nothing else to know.

I am all that is perceived, all that is imagined, everything is created within me. I am the beginning and end of all. I am the taste of water, the light of the sun, the sound of air, the smell of earth, and the heat of fire. I am life in the living. I am the eternal seed within all. In mankind, I am strength, devotion, and understanding.

I am eternal and unchanging, yet within me originates the forces of nature, directors of the illusionary layer of this world. But those who seek me, see beyond this layer. And those confused by the illusion, believing it to be all there is, are trapped within.

The one who knows me -- after many births, disciplined and full of understanding, devoted to me alone, knowing I am everything -- I consider to be my very self.

Others, confused and misled by illusion, devote

themselves to lesser goals. And to those seeking reward from their devotion, I grant it, though it be fleeting. Those that devote themselves to lesser goals, reach those lesser goals, while those devoted to me, reach me.

Those without understanding, believe the world they see is my entirety, unaware of my eternal and unchanging aspects. Veiled by a layer of illusion, I remain hidden to most. But unborn and enduring, I know all creatures that were, that are, and that will be.

At birth, all creatures are perplexed by the seemingly constant contradictions that arise from attraction and repulsion. But when devoted to me, they are freed from this confusion. By disciplining their thoughts, knowing me to be the sum of all, they know me at the time of death.

# Chapter 8

Seeking more detail, the Archer asks: How are you the sum of all, and how can the mentally disciplined know you at the time of death?

The Charioteer replies: I am the supreme everlasting energy that brings every creature into existence -- I am within all.

At the time of death, when departing the body, those who think of me, come to me -- of this there is no doubt. Whatever destination is in the mind at the time of death, is reached. Therefore, at all times think of me -- fight to keep me in your thoughts, and without doubt you will come to me.

Through the constant practice of focusing the mind and pruning the thoughts, one develops a steady mind with unwavering devotion, and upon departure, reaches the supreme state.

Listen, as I teach of the eternal state that is achieved through discipline. Training the mind to focus within, the disciplined are not confused by what the senses perceive. Those that utter the name of the infinite absolute, OM, and remember me upon departure, reach the supreme state.

I am easily reached by those focused on me alone, ever incorporating me into their thoughts. And having reached me and attained perfection, they no longer experience rebirth and the adversity of impermanence.

Entire worlds experience the cycle of creation and dissolution, but for those that reach me, the cycle ends. To the eternal, thousands of years are a brief moment. In the eternal scope, worlds are conceived at dawn and dismantled at dusk.

All creatures form from the unformed and dissolve back, again and again. But beyond this, resides the eternal and unchanging, that which does not perish even when all others cease to exist. This highest realm is where I reside, the source of all that is -- and those that attain it through unwavering devotion, remain here.

Listen as I tell you who is reborn and who is not. Those that follow the illuminated path to the absolute, find their way. Those that are lost in darkness, misled by illusion, remain. The man of discipline understands these paths, transcends the superficial, and ascends to the supreme abode.

# Chapter 9

The Charioteer continues: Because of your trust in me, I will reveal to you the way to be free of suffering. It is purifying, simple and understandable, and a joy to practice. Those without this understanding remain in the cycle of birth and death.

All things are dependent on me, and contained within me, but their totality does not define me. I exist beyond that which is revealed. And at the close of every cosmic cycle, all things dissolve into me, and I create them all again. By my direction, the laws of nature bring forth all things -- and by this process, the world turns. And as I perform this action, I remain unattached and indifferent to its outcome.

Those unaware of my eternal presence, knowing only what their flawed senses perceive, succumb to the influence of greed and cruelty. But those that know me as the source of all, training their senses to perceive only me, devote themselves to me through the living of their lives.

I am the ritual, the sacrifice, the hymn, and the offering. I am the father and mother, provider to all. I am the purifier and healer. I am what is to be known. I am OM and all that is sacred.

I am the journey and the goal. I am the comforter and supporter, friend, and witness. I am home. I am creation and cessation, the ground, and the inexhaustible seed. I am the provider of sun and rain. I am decay and that which endures. I am what is seen and what cannot be seen.

Those worshipping sacred tradition, striving for the rewards of heaven, reach their destination. But having enjoyed heavenly delights, they are reborn into the world of mortality and impermanence.

But to those focused on me, recognizing me in all things while seeking no other reward, I provide for.

No matter how or what men worship, I am the receiver of all worship, the enjoyer of all sacrifice. But knowing only my limited form, and not my true nature, men return to the cycle of birth and death. Worshippers of deities go to the deities, worshippers of ancestors go to the ancestors, worshippers of spirits go to the spirits, and worshippers of me come to me.

A single leaf or some water, offered to me with an attitude of devotion and gratitude, I readily accept. Indeed, whatever you do -- whatever you eat, whatever you give, whatever sacrifices you make -- do as an offering to me, and I will accept. In doing so, you will be freed from the bonds of these actions -- and with your essence unbound, you will come to me.

Impartial to all, I neither hate nor adore -- but those devoted to me, understand they are within me, and I am within them.

Even one whose deeds are villainous, must be considered pure when he worships me with complete devotion. His essence swiftly cleansed, he obtains lasting peace. Know that my followers never perish.

I welcome all who seek me, there are no distinctions. Whatever lineage, gender, or social status -- no matter how hated -- all may come to me.

In this fleeting world of adversity, devote yourself to what is welcoming and permanent. Train your thoughts to focus on me as the source of all, developing an attitude of gratefulness and admiration. With me as your goal, to me you will come.

# Chapter 10

The Charioteer continues: Mighty Archer, hear my words, he who knows me as unborn and without beginning, as the creator of worlds, he is free of delusion and corruption.

Understanding, freedom from delusion, patience, discipline, tranquility -- joy and suffering, existence and non-existence, fear and fearlessness -- mercy, kindness, contentment -- fame and infamy -- the various qualities of beings all come from me.

I am the common source from which all are descended. He who trains his thoughts upon this unity, is united with me through discipline.

Understanding that I am the origin of all, the wise keep me in their thoughts. Maintaining attitudes of appreciation and affection, their lives are lived as tributes to me, continually teaching and speaking of my ways -- they are content and filled with delight.

To those making me a persistent part of their lives, I grant the persistent understanding by which they come to me, illuminating the darkness of their ignorance with the light of wisdom.

Seeking more, the Archer inquires: You are the eternal all-pervading source of all, the supreme purifier and ultimate refuge. The ancient sages spoke this of you, and now you declare it yourself. I accept your words as truth -- but how may I know you in my thoughts, what form should I imagine, where do you reveal your presence in this world? Please tell me in detail of your power and its manifestation.

The Charioteer responds: As there is no end to my depths, I will reveal only a part of my nature.

I am the essence at the core of all living things. I am the beginning, middle, and end of being. I am awareness of life in the living. I am the comprehending mind among the senses.

Among lights, I am the blazing sun. Among lakes, I am the ocean. Among words, I am OM the eternal. Among offerings, I am focused meditation. Among the immovable, I am the Himalayas.

Among weapons, I am the thunderbolt. Among measures, I am time. Among knowledge, I am the realization of one's essence. Among debates, I am reasoning.

I am death, the destroyer and origin of what is to come. I am prestige, success, communication, memory, understanding, determination, and patience.

Among seasons, I am the flower bearing spring. Among risk-takers, I am chance. I am the brilliance of all that shines. I am victory and effort, and I am the goodness of the good.

Among those that punish, I am justice. Among those that strive, I am the path. Among secrets, I am silence. Among the wise, I am wisdom.

I am the seed of all life and sustainer of all that exists. There is no end to what I comprise, and what I've declared is only a fragment of my all-pervading nature. When witnessing an instance of excellence, know it to have sprung from a speck of my excellence.

But why inquire about such details? Know that I maintain the entirety of the universe, doing so with a fraction of my being.

# Chapter 11

The Archer makes a request: You have revealed to me the underlying nature of existence, ending my confusion. You have told me of the creation and destruction of all things that come into being, and of your eternal majesty. But is it possible for me to directly see this supreme all-pervading form of yours?

The Charioteer responds: Behold my thousands upon thousands of forms -- diverse in kind, color, and shape -- wonders never before seen. Witness the whole of the universe united within my body. To see all this, I will provide you with divine vision capable of perceiving the immensity of my being.

The old blind king's servant, also gifted with divine vision, describes this spectacle to the king: Having thus spoken, the Charioteer's miraculous form was revealed to the Archer.

Many mouths and eyes, all-devouring and all-seeing. Many wondrous ornaments, intricately beautiful. Many implements of death, ready and waiting. A brilliance no less than the light of a thousand blazing suns ascending into the sky.

The Archer witnessed the entirety of the universe with

its various divisions, all within the body of the supreme being. Overwhelmed with awe, with every hair raised on end, he bowed down his head, placed his hands together, and spoke.

The astonished Archer speaks: Within your body, I see all manner of beings. I see your infinite form with innumerable arms, bellies, mouths, and eyes, but no end, no middle, no beginning. I see your dazzling radiance shining brighter than the sun.

You are imperishable and supreme, the final resting place of the universe. You are the eternal guardian of action which must be done. You are the enduring essence within all.

Reaching beyond the sky, blazing with intense color, mouths salivating and eyes searing, I am shaken. Your mouths filled with savage fangs, leading to devouring flames, I am disoriented and frightened. Be merciful, as you are the only refuge.

I see in the distance my cousins and uncles, my teachers and friends, my brothers -- all rushing into your gruesome mouths filled with gnashing teeth. Caught between teeth, their heads crush to dust. As rivers rush into oceans, these men rush into your flaming mouths. As moths fly to flame, these men fly to their own destruction.

Devouring entire worlds, your fire fills the universe,

scorching with fierce radiance. And although I'm terrified, I wish to know and understand you. Who are you?

The Charioteer responds: I am time, the destroyer. Performing action that must be done, I consume the world. Even without your involvement, those involved in the battle before us will perish.

Therefore, great Archer, arise and fight. Conquer your enemies, oust your treacherous cousins and their supporters, and enjoy your kingdom. I have brought their lives to an end, you are but my instrument. Without trepidation, cut down your teachers and kinsmen that have been doomed by me. Fight and you shall be victorious.

The old blind king's servant, gifted with divine vision, describes the scene to the king: Trembling, hands together, the Archer bowed down fearfully and spoke, his voice faltering.

The Archer speaks: Within the world, you are both feared and adored. You are supreme, the creator, and the imperishable refuge. You are the knower of all and all that is to be known. You are all-pervading and the ultimate goal. You are wind and moon, fire and water, life and death, ancestor to all. Immeasurable in power, all achievement is yours! Within all, you are all.

Not knowing your greatness before this moment, I

dealt with you as a friend, careless and casual -- whatever disrespect I may have shown you, I beg for your forgiveness!

You are father to this world -- its teacher and object of devotion. I bow down before you, seeking your approval. Please show me patience -- as a father to his son, as a friend, and as one who is loved.

Having witnessed what has never been seen before, I am delighted, yet I am also overcome with fear at this shocking sight. Please show me your familiar form, so that I may be comforted.

The Charioteer responds: To you alone have I shown my supreme form -- a sight unreachable through sacrifice, study, charity, ritual, or asceticism. Be free of fear and regain your composure, see once again my familiar form.

The old blind king's servant, gifted with divine vision, describes the scene to the king: Having said this to the Archer, the Charioteer resumed his previous form, bringing comfort to the Archer.

The Archer speaks: Seeing your human form, I am myself again.

The Charioteer responds: Although difficult, you have seen my infinite form. Only through unyielding devotion can I be known, seen, and reached. He comes to me, who understands I am all that is, performing action for my sake, unattached, seeing me as the ultimate goal, and hateful to none.

# Chapter 12

The Archer inquires: Although you are all things, should I devote myself to this observable and fleeting world -- or concentrate on the imperishable realm that is without form?

The Charioteer responds: Most important, is sincere and unwavering devotion, with a mind ever aware of me.

Those focusing on the imperishable, persistently filtering the input of their senses, subduing preferences, delighting in the well-being of all -- they come to me. Although for those constrained within bodies, the formless absolute is difficult to attain. But dedicated to reaching me, surrendering their actions to me, devoted and constantly thinking of me -- I save them from the ocean of mortal existence.

Maintaining me in your thoughts, with me as the foundation of your understanding -- then in me will you live, of this there is no doubt. If you are unable to keep me in your thoughts, practice and refine your concentration with discipline. If you are unable to practice focusing your attention, then act without selfish intent, doing what need be done for my sake alone -- attaining perfection. If unable to do even this, become my instrument, accepting me as the driver, becoming my passenger, and seeing outcomes with equanimity, unconcerned with preferences or reward -- attaining peace.

Those near to me are without hate, friendly, kind, patient, without pride or selfishness, the same in pleasure or pain, content with any outcome, disciplined, determined -- and whose thoughts and understanding are based on me alone.

For those near to me, the world does not shun them, nor do they shun the world -- neither are they controlled by joy or anger, fear or anxiety.

Those near to me are without expectations, pure, diligent, and without concern or worry, renouncing the notion of self-reliance and independent self-directed action.

Those near to me do not exalt or disparage, grieve or desire, realizing there is no good or bad, only me. They are the same to friend and foe, respect and disrespect, heat and cold, delight and disgust -- being free of separateness and duality.

Those near to me see blame and praise as one, are restrained in speech, satisfied in any circumstance, and know me as home, having unwavering thoughts in an unshakable mind.

Those nearest to me are those that seek this enduring nourishment I have spoken of, dedicated to me above all.

# Chapter 13

The Charioteer continues: I am the essence within all bodies -- understanding the body and its essence is true knowledge.

The body is comprised of elements and self-awareness, solid form and intangible understanding, attraction and aversion, pleasure and pain, the forces of nature, as well as the perceiving senses.

Those with this knowledge are without pride, deceit, or hostility -- they are patient, honest, respectful, pure, unwavering, and self-controlled. They remain unswayed by what the senses perceive, lack self-importance, and perceive the futility of birth, pain, decay, sickness, and death. They do not cling to family or home, and are ever untroubled by the happenings of life. Dedicated in discipline, aligning with me rather than the crowd.

Persistent examination of the universal essence within all is true knowledge, the pathway to the eternal. Without beginning, beyond the qualities of existence and non-existence, with hands and feet in all places, eyes and ears on all sides, the perceiver of all that is sensed, this essence dwells within the world while enveloping all. Supporting all while being bound to none, unaffected by the forces of nature.

Being whole, beyond dualities, this essence is the internal and the external, the animate and inanimate, both distant and near, too complex to be known. Seemingly divided among beings, yet it is undivided. Sustaining all, yet their destroyer, creating everything anew.

This essence is the illumination of light, beyond darkness -- it is knowledge itself, the subject matter of knowledge, as well as the result of obtaining knowledge. This essence is within all. Those understanding the relationship of body and essence are united with me.

The visible world is born from the forces of nature, the cause and effect of all action. But it is the essence within, that experiences delight and discomfort -- and believing itself a part of nature, attaches to the visible world, becoming trapped within the cycle of rebirth.

This essence within the body is the observer, the adviser, the provider, and the experiencer -- it is the supreme universal essence permeating all bodies. Those realizing the entanglement of this essence within the forces of nature are not born again.

Some, through meditation, perceive the essence within -- some, by way of knowledge -- and some, through disciplined action. And some, hearing of this essence from those that directly perceive, devoted to what they have heard, even they cross beyond death.

Whatever is born, know it to be the union of body and spirit. And he who sees this universal essence existing equally within all, enduring even as the body fades, he truly sees. Seeing this essence everywhere, he is beyond suffering.

He who sees the forces of nature as the source of all action, and his eternal essence as the spectator, he truly sees. Perceiving the various forms of creatures as dispersed from a single source, he attains the underlying immortal truth.

Because the universal essence is without beginning and without features, it cannot act or become tainted, even though it dwells within the body. As a single sun illuminates the entire world, so too does the universal essence illuminate every being. Those understanding the divide between essence and body, and its release from the forces of nature, they reach an everlasting state.

# Chapter 14

The Charioteer continues: I will now tell of a knowledge by which the wise attain perfection. Relying on this knowledge, aligning with me, one is not reborn.

Nature is the soil in which I sow my seed. In the conception of every creature, nature is the womb and I, the father.

The forces of nature bind the eternal essence within the body. This restraining influence is divided into three aspects: understanding, passion, and stubbornness.

Understanding binds the essence with curiosity and delight, urging analysis of the visible world and contemplation of the pleasant.

Passion binds the essence with constant involvement through impulsive action, urging participation in the visible world through a continuous stream of wants.

Stubbornness binds the essence with a shortsighted perspective that is resistant to change, leading to confusion and misunderstanding, impeding knowledge of the world's true nature.

Understanding pursues happiness, passions induce action, and stubbornness obscures truth by a lack of deliberation.

Each of these three aspects can dominate within the body. When understanding dominates, the senses perceive the light of wisdom. When passions dominate, unsatisfiable cravings incite selfish action. When naive stubbornness dominates, a lack of depth creates carelessness and delusion.

Upon expiration of the body, the essence dominated by understanding enters into the pure place of those that truly see. When passions dominate, the essence is reborn among those that selfishly pursue their impulses -- and when shortsighted stubbornness dominates, the essence is reborn among the bewildered.

Action based on understanding reaps purity, action based on passion reaps pain, and action based on a stubborn perspective reaps ignorance.

Understanding produces wisdom, passions produce greed, and stubbornness produces folly.

Those with understanding rise, those with passion remain, and those mired in stubbornness sink.

When he perceives that all action is performed by the forces of nature, and realizes what lies beyond nature, he unites with me.

When the essence rises above the three forces of nature that govern the body, it is freed from birth and death, decay and distress, and attains the eternal.

The Archer inquires: What distinguishes one that rises above the forces of nature? How does he behave and how does he break free?

The Charioteer responds: He does not despise understanding, passion, or stubbornness when they appear, nor does he long for them when they disappear.

He is tolerant of the forces of nature. Knowing it is nature alone that acts, he remains a peaceful audience, unwavering.

Realizing the unity of all, he is satisfied within himself. Pleasure and pain, pleasant and unpleasant, praise and blame, honor and disgrace, friend and foe, jewel and rock -- seeing beyond dualities, perceiving all things equally, he neither covets nor avoids. Abandoning the idea of self-determination, he rises above the forces of nature.

Lovingly devoted to me, unbound from the forces of nature, he is suited to blend with the imperishable, entering into the eternal home of essential action and absolute bliss.

# Chapter 15

The Charioteer continues: Within the visible world, senses captivated, the essence is bound to action by the forces of nature. Cut these imaginary bonds with the ax of detachment -- seek the path of no return, the path to the originator of all.

No longer deluded by a sense of independence, without desire for selfish gain or personal accomplishment, lacking attachment to wants -- those upon this path are dedicated to the supreme essence -- free from dualities, they reach the eternal, they come to me.

My fragment is the core, the universal essence within, around which forms the body, vessel of the mind and senses. When exiting a body to enter another, like fragrance lingering in the air, remnants accompany this essence.

Hearing, seeing, touching, tasting, smelling, and thinking -- this essence engages with the perceptible world. The deluded do not see this essence within the body, only those with the eye of wisdom see it.

Clouded with impurities, the undisciplined cannot see, though they may try. Only those purified through persistent practice see the essence within.

I am the brilliance of the sun that illuminates the world, vitalizing plant and animal with my energy, providing nourishment and the means to sustain life.

From me, comes the memory and understanding within all beings. I am the theme of all sacred texts, their author, the knower of their truths.

Within each being, there is the perishable and the imperishable. The perishable is all that grows within the world, the imperishable is all that does not change. And beyond those, there is the supreme universal essence that sustains the totality.

I am preeminent, beyond the perishable and imperishable. He who knows me so, knows all. By understanding this lesson, he attains wisdom and fulfillment.

# Chapter 16

The Charioteer continues: Without fear or negativity, without anger or brutality, without jealousy or pride, detached, forgiving, gentle and kind, serene, sincere, steady, disciplined, ever watching the mind and studying my ways -- these are the qualities of those closest to me, leading to release from the cycle of birth and death.

Deceitful, arrogant, hostile, cruel, and ignorant -- these are the qualities of those furthest from me, leading to bondage within the cycle of rebirth.

Now, hear more of those with attributes that lead away from me: when action is necessary, they are stationary -- when stillness is required, they are active. They lack understanding and truth, claiming the world is brought about through the mingling of independent lust-driven acts, denying the world's interwoven oneness. They are lost within their vain perspective, ever devising ways to fulfill their cravings, without regard for the entirety of the world.

Surrendering to their insatiable appetite, they are polluted with hypocrisy and self-importance, their deluded ideas inciting their foolish actions.

Confident that life's purpose is the fulfillment of their cravings, they remain obsessed with their wants until death. Bound by hundreds of wants and wishes, driven by greed and frustration, they cunningly endeavor to accumulate resources in an attempt to obtain satisfaction.

"I have gained today, fulfilling my wish, it is now mine, and even more will come to be mine. I have defeated my adversary, I will conquer all who oppose me -- am I not a god, enjoyer of my own success, powerful and well-pleased. I am wealthy and well-born, without equal, I will hand out charity, pleased with my generosity and virtue." This they say, deluded by their ignorance.

Entangled by their confusion, and addicted to gratification, they fall far from me. Self-centered, stubborn, and prideful of their possessions -- they perform exhibitions of cooperation and sacrifice in name only, disregarding their intended purpose.

Confident in their individuality, trusting their narrow perspective and their desires, compelled by discontent -- they despise me. Entering into the wombs of those furthest from me, they remain within the cycle of birth and death, sinking to the lowest state.

Lust, anger, and greed serve as pathways to this lowest state -- reject their influence -- seek me, and reach the highest state.

But those that follow their desires, rejecting my path, fail to attain happiness or the highest state. Let my teachings guide you within this world.

# Chapter 17

The Archer inquires: What of those that attempt devotion, yet lack the knowledge -- what is their nature?

The Charioteer responds: One's degree of devotion is based on one's nature. Those with a nature of pure understanding, devote themselves to what lies beyond their senses. Those with a passionate nature, devote themselves to that which they believe influences the world of the senses. Those with a stubborn nature, devote themselves to the past.

Those driven to harshly punish and abuse their bodies are tormenting the essence dwelling within -- believing their bodies to be the pinnacle of existence, they are far from me.

The food one eats -- as well as one's dedication, discipline, and capacity for giving -- are each expressed by the three forces of nature. Listen, as I tell of these distinctions.

Those with a nature of pure understanding gravitate to foods promoting wellness and vitality, providing delight and nourishment -- food that is appetizing, having a texture that is easily consumed. Those with a passionate nature gravitate to foods promoting discomfort, having a texture or taste that is a challenge to consume. Those with a stubborn nature gravitate to foods that are stale or rotting.

Dedication of effort and resources to what is necessary, without concern for reward, arises from the nature of pure understanding. Dedication of effort and resources for the sake of appearances and the attainment of reward, arises from the passionate nature. And the squandering of effort and resources, lacking focus, arises from the stubborn nature.

Acting in accordance with the eternal path -- respecting wisdom, purity, and trustworthiness -- restraining lusts and violent outbursts -- this is discipline of the body. Speaking kindly and gently, with sincerity, and speaking of my ways -- this is discipline of speech. Silencing thoughts, cultivating mental tranquility, and pruning polluted ideas -- this is discipline of the mind.

Practicing these three disciplines without expectation of reward, is the nature of pure understanding. Practicing these disciplines for the sake of reputation and reward, is the nature of passion, the results being volatile and brief. Practicing these disciplines by way of self-harm or harm to others, is the nature of unthinking stubbornness.

Giving without expectation of receiving, in the spirit of

wholeness, during the appropriate time and place, to a fitting recipient -- this charity lies within the nature of pure understanding. Giving with reluctance or while seeking a return -- this charity lies within the passionate nature. Giving at the wrong time or place, to an unfitting recipient, scornfully -- this charity lies within the nature of unthinking stubbornness.

Dedication of one's efforts, discipline of one's body and mind, and the giving of one's resources, begin with the recognition of OM, the eternal and all-pervading. Without selfless devotion to the whole, the practices of dedication, discipline, and charity have no value here or hereafter.

# Chapter 18

The Archer inquires: I want to know the difference between abstaining from action and the relinquishment of its reward.

The Charioteer responds: There is abstaining from action brought about by urges, and there is the abandonment of the fruits of action.

Some say that all action leads away from me, while others say that certain actions -- devotion, discipline, and helping others -- should always be performed. Hear now, what I say.

Acts of devotion, discipline, and contribution are not to be avoided, but performed -- they purify those upon my path. But even these acts should be performed without concern for a favorable outcome -- or believing oneself to be the instigator of these acts.

Avoiding any act that is fitting to one's character, leads away from me. Avoiding acts due to a lack of consideration, is the nature of stubbornness -- and avoiding acts due to the fear of pain, is the nature of passion and produces no benefit. But performing acts that must be done, in harmony with one's characteristics, without personalizing, is the nature of pure understanding.

Those upon my path, determined to reach me, neither avoid the unpleasant nor cling to the pleasant. And to maintain the physical body, one must act -- only the selfish motivation for action is renounceable, not action itself.

The fruit of all action -- whether pleasant, unpleasant, or mixed -- accumulates and remains even after death. But for those that renounce the fruit of action, acting without selfish intent, there is no accumulation.

Listen, as I describe the five elements comprising every action. The physical body and its intangible witness, the perceptions and urges, and the universal narrative -- whatever activity is performed through the flesh, speech, or thought -- these five elements are the root.

Seeing himself as the sole author of action, a man misunderstands, and does not truly see. But free from a sense of individuality, with clear understanding, uncorrupted by selfish desire, even if he brings about the death of others, he is not their killer, nor is he bound by his actions to the cycle of rebirth.

Awareness, the subject of that awareness, and the experiencer of awareness, provide the motivation for action. The motivation, the act, and the performer, are the components of action.

Awareness, action, and the performer fall under the influence of the forces of nature. Hear now, the distinction of each.

An awareness that perceives the universal essence within all, undivided within the divided, stems from an understanding nature. An awareness that perceives the variety of life as unconnected, stems from a passionate nature. And an awareness that narrowly perceives only a single part as the whole, stems from a stubborn nature.

Action that is necessary, performed impartially, without selfish motive, without infatuation or distaste -- comes from an understanding nature. Action performed for the fulfillment of wants and prideful accomplishment, bringing unwarranted strain -- comes from a passionate nature. Action that is based in misunderstanding, performed without consideration -- comes from a stubborn nature.

The performer that lacks an attachment to outcomes, unaffected by success or failure, is enthusiastic and undaunted, and not self-centered -- acts from a nature of pure understanding. The performer incited by emotion, craving reward, greedy, cruel and corrosive, and swept away by joy and grief -- acts from a passionate nature. The performer that is reckless and inappropriate, obstinate and immature, deceitful and pessimistic, sluggish -- acts from a stubborn nature.

Hear now, the distinctions of understanding and dedication, each according to the forces of nature.

The understanding that is pure, knows which actions are necessary and when to perform them, what not to fear, what binds the essence, and what sets it free. The understanding that is selfish and impulsive, having a passionate perspective, misses what is wholesome and necessary. The understanding that is recklessly stubborn, continuously twisting light into darkness, interprets that which is unwholesome as necessary and nourishing, believing things to be what they are not.

Dedication sustained by discipline of the mind, descends from the nature of pure understanding. Dedication sustained by desire for reward from one's actions, descends from the nature of self-obsessed passion. Dedication sustained by thoughtless inflexibility, descends from the nature of stubbornness.

Hear now, the three distinctions of happiness, which when maintained, brings enjoyment and an end to discontent. Happiness that arises from a clear comprehension of one's essence, which is at first bitter, but sweet in the end, lies within the nature of pure understanding. Happiness that arises from the fulfillment of wants, which is at first sweet, but bitter in the end, lies within the nature of passion. Happiness that arises from inactivity and carelessness, masquerading as sweet, yet bitter from beginning to end, lies within the nature of unthinking stubbornness.

No being is free from the forces of nature. Advisers, guardians, industrialists, and craftsmen -- the divisions of society and corresponding duties are determined by the innate characteristics found within each.

Serenity, self-control, disciplined practice, incorruptibility, patience, sincerity, rationality, understanding, and devotion -- by their nature, this is the duty of advisers.

Courage, enthusiasm, strength, proficiency, perseverance, generosity, and selfless protection -- by their nature, this is the duty of guardians.

Development and management of society's resources -- by their nature, this is the duty of industrialists.

Craftwork and artistry, sculptors of society's resources -- by their nature, this is the duty of craftsmen.

Each one devoted to his own duty, attains perfection. By utilizing his innate characteristics in the selfless performance of duty, he becomes like the all-pervading creator. Even duty performed imperfectly, is better than performing another's duty perfectly.

Aligned with his nature, performing his duty, he is never far from me. Even if flawed, he should not abandon action suited for his nature, for all activities are permeated with flaws, just as fire is permeated with smoke.

Free from an independent sense of self, disciplined, no longer cherishing wants -- he attains a perfect state that transcends the consequences of action. Hear now, how upon achieving perfection, he attains supreme understanding.

Through practice, he purifies his understanding -- he disregards input from the senses, disregards attraction and aversion, and disregards influence from others. Through practice, he regulates his diet, regulates his speech and body and mind, maintains awareness and focus, disregarding the influence of emotions. He disregards any sense of separateness and possession -- he disregards hostility, pride, desire, anger, and selfishness -- fostering tranquility. And from this discipline, he develops a supreme understanding.

And having attained this supreme understanding, he does not experience longing or loss. Seeing all things the same, he realizes all devotion is to me. And through this devotion, he comes to know me -- and having known me, he merges into my essence.

Performing action, sheltered within me, harmonized with my nature, he reaches the eternal home.

Within your thoughts, regard me as appreciator of all action. Through reason and practice, maintain focus on me. With me in your thoughts, you will go beyond all dilemmas. But if your thoughts dwell upon yourself, then you are lost.

If in your self-obsessed thoughts, you decide, "I will not fight" -- your decision is worthless -- your nature will compel you to act. In your delusion, you refuse to act, but your nature requires action -- thus you will participate, despite your misguided wishes.

The forces of nature drive all beings to act, setting pace and direction. Take comfort in their guidance, and obtain everlasting peace.

Thus I have revealed this teaching, invisible to the senses -- consider it fully, then act as you will.

Hear now, my final words. Keeping me in your thoughts at all times, devoted, relinquishing all actions to me and accepting me as your guide -- you will come to me.

Realizing that all actions stem from me, I shield you from their consequences.

This teaching is only for those ready and willing to receive it. And he who shares this teaching appropriately, surely comes to me -- there is no greater service to me than this.

And he who studies this dialog, I consider devoted to

me. And he who listens to it with acceptance, moves closer to me.

Do you understand what I have said? Is your confusion gone?

The Archer responds: My confusion is gone, I see clearly, I am without doubt. You have spoken, now I will act.

The old blind king's servant, speaks to the king: As I listened to this wondrous conversation, my hair stood on end. By the divine vision granted to me, I heard this supreme teaching revealed by the Creator himself. O King, as I remember this sacred dialog, I am filled with delight. And as I recall the astonishing endless form of the Creator, I overflow with joy.

Wheresoever the spirit of this Archer and his Charioteer is rooted, I believe serendipity, success, happiness, and goodness, spring forth.

### The End

# Chapter 1 Commentary

It's been a long chain of abuses leveled against the Archer and his brothers by their cousins, the sons of the blind king. The Archer's eldest brother is the rightful heir to the throne, but the blind king has other ideas, wanting his own eldest son to inherit the kingdom. And accordingly, the blind king's son does what he can to seize the throne from his eldest cousin -- including treachery, humiliation, and attempted murder. This ruthless behavior culminates in a war, dividing the family and their supporters, placing them on opposite sides of a battlefield.

The Archer is saddened by this because across the field he sees his eldest family member, dearly beloved, he sees his teacher, deeply respected, and he sees his cousins and uncles, playmates and caretakers since childhood. So distraught is this Archer, that he falls to his knees in tears.

# Chapter 2 Commentary

Unwilling to fight, the Archer asks his Charioteer for advice. The Charioteer encourages the Archer to fight and presents some ideas to help him reshape the way he thinks about the situation.

The Charioteer starts by introducing the idea of rebirth. As we grow older, certain characteristics remain with us -- so no matter our age, there exists a continuity of identity -- we're still ourselves. The Charioteer proposes that this concept also applies to life and death: when we die, we simply discard our bodily shell and inhabit a new one. So death is not a tragic event, but a mere change of wardrobe.

The Charioteer continues, mentioning the ambiguous nature of the visible world. What the senses perceive, is just a parade of stimuli -- illusions that engage the senses -- a brief show of light and sound, taste and touch. But below that surface, there lies an unchanging reality that is beyond human perception. And within this eternal underlying realm, our essence exists forever, beyond harm.

The Charioteer then mentions the necessity of following one's natural tendencies without the influence of imagined outcomes. In other words, suppressing our impulses in order to avoid a seemingly unpleasant outcome provides temporary relief, but ultimately ends in dissatisfaction.

He advises that we accept life's narrative and perform our role. We should not shy away from life, but engage in it, doing our part by following our impulses -- and through our active participation, we obtain satisfaction.

Reward or punishment, success or failure -- the outcome doesn't matter -- he suggests that we not attempt to control outcomes, but control our attitude pertaining to outcomes. So whatever happens, we remain satisfied -- and we achieve this steady attitude through practice.

For this practice, we train our minds to interpret our perceptions in a lighthearted manner -- not obsessing over the input of the senses. We remind ourselves that the senses cannot discern lasting truth, only fleeting illusion. And accordingly, fear and frustration become relics in the face of this new understanding.

Thoughts continually enter our minds, but we don't dwell on them -- we remain undisturbed by their turbulence, attaining calmness and joyfulness.

# Chapter 3 Commentary

The Archer wonders, if training the mind is a means to end his suffering, why must he still participate in the battle? Can't he skip the battle and just train his mind?

The Charioteer explains that action is a necessary condition for living in the world -- just to maintain the body, action is unavoidable. Additionally, impulses from within force our participation. Because of this, inaction and the restraint of action are not possible in the long-term, they are pointless.

But although we are compelled to act, we can detach ourselves from these acts. By using reason to convince ourselves that we are not the true instigators of action, that we are only witnesses, we end our delusion and decouple ourselves from the actions we perform.

Following along life's narrative, performing our role without complaint -- this is the path to fulfillment. Reject obsession for the pleasant and reject hatred of the unpleasant -- as they attach our essence to the visible world.

Ambitions and goals, wishing for specifics -- these bring frustration and confusion, causing us to behave out of character. But by following our nature, and training our mind not to cling to what the senses perceive, we become ourselves, our essence shines brightly.

# Chapter 4 Commentary

The Charioteer mentions that he taught this knowledge to the ancients, but it faded over time. Seeing his Charioteer as a man similar in age to himself, the Archer is confused by this. The Charioteer informs the Archer that he remembers all of his previous incarnations, life after life -- suggesting he is not what he appears to be.

The Charioteer continues, stating that he enters into the world when it is in turmoil, re-establishing balance, preserving the best aspects while eliminating the worst -- becoming a beacon for all to strive towards.

The Charioteer asserts that those who strive, following a path towards fulfillment, will reach their destination. No longer trusting their senses, they no longer experience fear and frustration -- without expectations, they are without discontent -- performing as their nature dictates, without selfish motivation or external influence, they are free and unattached to this world. Devoted to acting without attachment, they find peace.

# Chapter 5 Commentary

The Archer, still trying to understand, asks whether his discontent is best relieved through engaging with the world, or by adjusting the way he thinks. The Charioteer says both are necessary.

We can shape our thoughts: weed out negativity, focus on the unity of all things, and repeatedly remind ourselves that we are not the originators of action. We are passengers, not drivers -- and understanding this, it becomes pointless to obsess over manipulating the world or to focus on outcomes. And remembering that we perceive the world through faulty senses, we know we cannot rely on those perceptions.

By accepting our nature, we find peace. By knowing what we are, we see everything and everyone as equal, united by a common core. We cannot separate the whole, praising the pleasant while criticizing the unpleasant -- we must appreciate the underlying unity of all, and in doing so, we attain tranquility.

Separateness is an illusion, so obsessing on a single part of this world is not a means to fulfillment. And because of our limited senses, training our thoughts is the only way to perceive this wholeness and know joy.

Desire, doubt, fear, and anger surge through our minds -- but if we dedicate ourselves to disregarding their importance, and focus on the positive aspects in all things, we are left with calm and joy -- we attain peace and freedom.

# Chapter 6 Commentary

The Charioteer now speaks of the discipline for attaining peace and freedom: avoid wishing for particular outcomes and abandon selfishness, and from that foundation, we are to act how our impulses direct us, doing what we're compelled to do.

Life provides the grounds on which we practice this discipline. And when we improve through practice, no longer trying to satisfy our selfish wants, we attain tranquility, engaging lightheartedly with the world.

Our reasoning mind can cultivate joy or misery -- what we focus on determines our level of enjoyment. So no matter the external conditions, a disciplined mind remains the same. Although the visible world constantly attempts to entangle the senses, the disciplined mind is beyond reach, seeing all things without distinction, knowing everything as equal.

The Charioteer continues by describing a form of practice useful for weakening the external world's influence on the mind. Remaining motionless, observing the mind, focus on that which endures (such as the breath), and when fleeting thoughts or input from the senses surface, return focus to that which endures. A disciplined mind finds peace.

Also useful for the practice of discipline, is the regulation of diet, sleep, activity, and recreation. And when disciplined, without wants or obsessions, our essence is revealed.

The realization that the senses cannot perceive truth, brings lasting joy -- we are no longer troubled by life's drama.

With practice, we can cut our ties to misery by maintaining an unfocused view of the external. We can practice by not allowing our mind to obsess on frivolous wants, and by using reason to refute the input of our senses. Over time, this brings tranquility.

Sensing when the mind wanders down a negative path, bringing awareness back to the mind itself, not following those unfavorable thoughts -- this is a disciplined mind.

No longer influenced by the senses, perceiving all things equally, we realize our fellowship with all. Seeing our shared essence everywhere, we are never lost.

But hearing the Charioteer speak of a calm mind perplexes the Archer. His mind is overwhelmed by his racing thoughts, so to him, the idea of restraining his thoughts seems impossible. The Charioteer agrees that the mind is difficult to control, but assures the Archer that it's possible with dedicated practice.

The Archer then wonders what happens if he fails to discipline his mind, will his failure even affect him after death? The Charioteer reassures the Archer that any progress he makes in this life will follow him to the next.

Life after life, if we strive towards perfection by training our minds, we eventually achieve it -- and upon perfection, we seamlessly merge into the infinite, born no more.

# Chapter 7 Commentary

The Charioteer now reveals more of his true nature to the Archer, aspects that are not readily seen or heard.

The Charioteer represents the entirety of the universe, in human-like form, speaking to the Archer. He describes himself as the sum of everything: all that lies within the perceptible world, as well as its eternal foundation.

Because his underlying nature is imperceptible to our senses, it can only be known within our thoughts. And upon realizing his pervading presence, we are able to utilize him as the beacon that guides us upon our path towards a state of perfection.

Because our senses cannot perceive beyond the visible world, many believe it to be all there is -- but in doing so, they are trapped within it. Through practice, those that maintain the eternal unseen aspects of the universe in their thoughts are no longer trapped.

# Chapter 8 Commentary

The Charioteer says that whatever destination is in our minds as we die, we reach it. When our thoughts are focused on this world, we remain within this world -- our thoughts attach us to it. So by focusing on what lies beyond the senses, we can reach a permanent state.

By using reason to dismantle what our senses perceive, removing the limitations they place upon us, convincing ourselves that absolute truth cannot be seen by our eyes, by incorporating eternal ideas within our thinking -- we can reach the state of perfection, escaping the struggle of rebirth.

We achieve this through practice. Those lost in the fog of superficiality remain, those that strive toward the light, seeking clarity, attain it.

# Chapter 9 Commentary

The creation of the universe and everything it contains is done without passion, without selfishness, without attachment to a particular outcome -- it is simply done because the role of a creator is to create.

Those believing the visible world to be all there is, succumb to the influence of greed and cruelty -- unaware that all things within this world stem from a single source and are of equal value.

Those focused on what lies beyond the senses, not seeking imagined rewards, are without hardship. Devoted to realizing the source of all, devoted to seeing this source within all, and devoted to developing an attitude of gratefulness to this source of all -- for those so devoted, suffering comes to an end.

Everything you do, think of it as a form of devotion to what created us. When we consider the living of our lives as a form of devotion, as an offering of appreciation, we are no longer tied to our actions. No longer tied to our actions, we are without attachment, we are free.

The Charioteer says: In this fleeting world of adversity, devote yourself to what is welcoming and permanent.

Train your thoughts to focus on me as the source of all, developing an attitude of gratefulness and admiration. With me as your goal, to me you will come.

# Chapter 10 Commentary

Everything descends from a common source -- maintaining this idea within our thoughts, we unite with the whole. And when we develop an appreciation for this world, we become content.

The Archer, still anchored in the realm of the senses, wonders where in this world the Charioteer reveals his power and in what form he should be envisioned.

The Charioteer, representing the entirety of the infinite universe, explains that his description is literally without end, so he describes only a fraction of his presence. But in closing, the Charioteers says that such detail is unnecessary, just know that he is everything and maintains the world with only a fraction of his being.

# Chapter 11 Commentary

The Archer, still captivated by his senses, asks if he can see the actual all-pervading eternal form of the Charioteer.

The Charioteer grants this request, providing the Archer with a divine vision capable of perceiving his immensity. What's revealed, is a distressing sight for the Archer. It is not only grand, but gruesome. In the distance, he sees the participants on both sides of the battlefield, his family, relentlessly crushed and consumed by gnashing teeth within flaming mouths.

Although terrified, the Archer seeks to know more. The Charioteer explains that he is time, the destroyer -- and even without the Archer's involvement, the men on the battlefield would perish. The narrative of life has brought an end to the lives of these men, the Archer is merely the instrument that fulfills this sequence of events. And with that, the Charioteer urges the Archer to accept his role in fighting this battle.

The Archer, now comprehending the immensity of what's before him, trembles. Overwhelmed, he asks to see his Charioteer's familiar form once again.

The Charioteer, now in human-like form, says: Only

through unyielding devotion can I be known. Understand that I am everything, and hate nothing -- perform your role for my sake, and remain unbound -- seek me as your goal, and find me.

# Chapter 12 Commentary

The Archer wonders whether he should focus on this observable world or the infinite unseen realm.

The Charioteer responds: It is a challenge for embodied beings to contemplate that which is eternal and without form. But for those that focus on what doesn't end, overcoming the influence of their senses and their preferences, celebrating the well-being of all -- they reach the eternal state through their dedicated practice.

The Charioteer continues: Keep me in your thoughts by making me the foundation of your understanding. To do so, practice focusing your attention -- act without selfish intent, do not seek to benefit -- see all outcomes as equal -- think of yourself as my instrument -- and through this practice, attain peace.

The Charioteer says: those that see all things as me, are near to me. Seeing everyone as me, they are without hate or selfishness, they are kind and patient. Seeing me in every result, they are satisfied with any outcome. Seeing me in every circumstance, they are not influenced by anger or anxiety. Seeing me as the sustainer of life, they abandon the belief of self-determination. Seeing only me, they are without dualities -- there is no good or bad, there is only me.

Those nearest to me know me as home, and are at all times content.

# Chapter 13 Commentary

The Charioteer says he is the eternal essence within all. And if everyone is of the same core, then what use is pride, deceit, or hostility? There are no autonomous individuals, just parts of a whole. When we think of ourselves as pieces of an infinite universe, we lack self-importance -- we see birth, sickness, and death as unimportant. The happenings of life just happen and we remain unperturbed.

When we strive to realize this eternal core, we come to understand it as the true perceiver of our senses -- the world's inhabitants comprise its many hands and feet, its many eyes and ears.

Containing the entirety of the universe, this eternal essence is beyond divisions and dualities, it is whole. And when we understand our relationship with the whole, we are united with it.

The visible world is formed from the forces of nature, but it is the essence within that experiences, observing the ongoings of life. And when this essence believes itself to be a part of nature, it becomes trapped within it, life after life. But upon realizing its entanglement, this embodied essence merges with the eternal, never to be born again.

Through dedication, the internal essence can be perceived in the mind. Whatever is born, is the union of nature and spirit, an eternal essence existing equally within all -- the forces of nature are the source of all action, and this spirit the spectator -- maintaining these ideas in our thoughts, we can go beyond suffering, reaching an everlasting state.

# Chapter 14 Commentary

The Charioteer now explains how an embodied essence, through its confusion, is bound by the forces of nature within the cycle of rebirth.

An embodied essence, in its observation of life, can become attached to life's interesting and endearing aspects -- or it can become attached to fulfilling wants -- or it can become attached to an inflexible view of life. And when attached, the embodied essence is trapped within the cycle of rebirth.

By realizing it is beyond nature, the essence is freed from distress and rebirth and merges with the eternal. An unattached essence does not despise the influence of nature, nor long for it. Knowing that nature alone instigates action, abandoning the idea of self-determination, this essence remains a calm and content audience.

Beyond dualities, seeing all things equally, this essence neither covets nor avoids -- realizing it is whole, this essence is satisfied. Unbound from the forces of nature, this essence blends with the imperishable.

# Chapter 15 Commentary

The embodied essence can become captivated by the visible world, trapping itself within a cycle of rebirth.

But when the embodied essence realizes its origin, no longer believing itself independent, no longer attached to personal gain or accomplishment -- this detached essence returns to the eternal.

That force which creates and sustains the universe is the core within all bodies -- and through every eye, it sees the world.

Only a mind purified by persistent practice can perceive this eternal core.

This eternal core within all transient bodies, is the universe itself, as well as that which lies beyond, without form, imperishable and unchanging.

# Chapter 16 Commentary

Fearful, angry, cruel, deceitful, jealous, arrogant -- these are qualities of those trapped within the cycle of rebirth. Seeing all things as independent, they lack understanding of the interwoven world.

Chasing cravings without regard for others, they act foolishly within the world, polluted by hypocrisy and self-importance. Believing life's purpose to be the fulfillment of wants, they remain obsessed until death, forever seeking satisfaction, bound by hundreds of wants and wishes.

Believing themselves separate and capable of individual achievement, their conceit propels them far from the whole. Self-centered, feigning cooperation for their own benefit, they fall far from perfection, sinking deeper within the cycle of rebirth.

Serving as pathways to this lowest state, reject the influence of lust, anger, and greed. With these teachings as your guide, seek the path to perfection and happiness.

# Chapter 17 Commentary

The stubborn attempt to maintain the past, the passionate attempt to influence the perceptible world, but those with understanding devote themselves to what lies beyond the senses. Those believing the body to be the summit of existence, lack understanding.

Even with food, the stubborn consume what is stale and unwholesome, the passionate gravitate towards foods challenging to consume, but those with understanding consume what is nourishing and appetizing.

The stubborn lack focus, squandering resources and effort, the passionate seek reward and empty praise, but those with understanding seek to uphold what is necessary, unconcerned for reward.

Restraining lusts and outbursts, this is discipline of the body. Speaking gently with sincerity of what is genuine, this is discipline of speech. Pruning polluted ideas and stilling thoughts, this is discipline of mind.

The stubborn practice this discipline by abusing the body, tormenting the essence within. The passionate practice this discipline for the sake of reputation and reward, but those with understanding practice this discipline without concern for reward.

The stubborn give scornfully at the wrong time and place, to the unfitting. The passionate give reluctantly, seeking something in return. But those with understanding give to those that lack, in the spirit of wholeness and without expectations, at the appropriate time and place.

Dedication, discipline, and giving begin with recognition of the whole -- or else they are worthless -- in this world or any other.

# Chapter 18 Commentary

Those with understanding do not avoid the unpleasant or cling to the pleasant, but perform what must be done, in harmony with their nature, without believing themselves the instigator of these acts. It is a misunderstanding to see oneself as the sole author of action.

Action is unavoidable, only selfish intent is renounceable. Acts performed without thought of selfish gain, without a sense of individuality, do not bind one's essence within the cycle of rebirth.

The stubborn reject action due to a lack of consideration, the passionate reject action due to the fear of pain, but those with understanding do not reject action befitting their character, ever accepting what must be done.

The stubborn perceive only a single part of the totality as the whole, the passionate perceive the totality as unconnected divisions, but those with understanding perceive the same underlying essence within all, indivisible.

The stubborn, inappropriate and pessimistic, perform actions rooted in misunderstanding and thoughtlessness. The passionate, incited by emotion, selfish and cruel, perform actions rooted in desire and ambition. But those with understanding, unattached to outcomes, perform actions rooted in impartiality and altruism, unswayed by infatuation or revulsion and free of selfishness.

The stubborn perspective twists dark into light, seeing the corrosive as necessary and nourishing. The passionate perspective, impulsive and focused on itself, misses what is wholesome and necessary. But the perspective that comes from understanding knows what is necessary and what not to fear, discerning what binds the essence and what sets it free.

Stubborn dedication is sustained by thoughtless inflexibility, passionate dedication is sustained by desire for reward, but for those with understanding, dedication is sustained by a disciplined mind.

The stubborn receive happiness from what masquerades as sweet, yet is bitter from beginning to end. The passionate receive happiness from what is at first sweet, but bitter in the end. Those with understanding receive happiness from what is at first bitter, but sweet in the end.

Advisers, guardians, industrialists, and craftsmen -- the divisions of society with their corresponding duties, determined by the innate characteristics found within each.

The duty of advisers is to provide reasoning and understanding to society, utilizing their self-discipline, sincerity, serenity, and patience. The duty of guardians is selfless protection of society, utilizing their courage, strength, proficiency, and perseverance. The duty of industrialists is the development and management of society's resources. The duty of craftsmen is the materialization of society's resources through craftwork and artistry.

Even if performed imperfectly, those selflessly devoted to their duty, aligned with their nature, become like the all-pervading creator and attain perfection.

Free of an independent sense of self, unattached to wants, disciplined -- within this perfect state, one transcends the consequences of action.

Attain understanding through discipline. With practice, disregard input from the senses, disregard attraction and aversion, and disregard influence from others. With practice, disregard the influence of emotions -- disregard hostility, pride, desire, anger, and selfishness -- fostering tranquility. With practice, disregard any sense of separateness and possession. With practice, regulate diet, speech, body, and mind. With practice, maintain awareness and focus.

Those that attain this understanding do not experience longing or loss, seeing all things the same. And from this unity, they merge with the infinite. Those that focus on themselves are lost.

Deciding not to act is worthless, as nature compels action -- following one's nature is inevitable. The forces of nature drive all beings to act, take comfort in their guidance. Knowing that all action stems from these forces, be free of their consequences.

This teaching is invisible to the senses, it must be considered solely within the mind. This teaching is not readily available, but only for those ready and willing to receive it.

There is no greater service than to share this teaching appropriately -- and for those that listen and accept this teaching, they move closer to perfection.

# Afterword

A very brief and sensationalist synopsis of the Bhagavad Gita could be: God convinces a man to murder his family.

It's true that Arjuna is within the middle of a battlefield in opposition to many of his mentors and family members. It's also true that he's hesitant to participate in this battle because he doesn't want to kill them. And it's also true that his charioteer, Krishna, God-incarnate, does spend the entire time convincing Arjuna that it's okay to take part in this battle.

If this is all true, what's so enlightening about this story and what relevance does it have to our lives in the modern world?

A truer synopsis could be: God helps a man to cope with life. No matter how Arjuna felt about it, the battle was going to happen — and because he had family on both sides, because of the culture he was in, and because his nature would compel him to take part — Arjuna's participation was inevitable.

So what Krishna did, was to help Arjuna accept his role, to feel better about engaging in this battle. Krishna explained life in a way that removed Arjuna's misery and fear. And as witnesses to this conversation, we can utilize the same ideas to better cope with our own lives — and not just cope, but end our suffering, attain peace and happiness, and tame our turbulent minds.

Made in the USA
Middletown, DE
19 October 2022